Wal=Militia

Wal=Militia

THE CONSPIRACY OF WAL-MART
AND THE GOVERNMENT:
A NATIONAL REPORT

Grant Lee

To order additional copies of this book, contact:
Xlibris Corporation
1-888-795-4274
www.Xlibris.com
Orders@Xlibris.com
24794

Contents

Introduction

In the summer of 1998, I was twenty three years old and took a job at Merchant Security working as a security guard in Rogers, Arkansas, which lies comfortably in the northwest corner of that odd shaped state, and in the middle of the eternally green Ozarks—Hillbilly country.

I was employed for a mere five dollars and thirty five cents an hour, but thoroughly loved the job because I had the pleasure of seeing to the well being of many people and places. Among them were colleges, convenience stores, malls, manufacturing plants, car lots, boat marinas, and many, many others. It was fun and I really never had any major problems that I had to contend with, except for the occasional noise maker.

A couple of weeks into my job I was asked to take a security patrol car and guard the construction site of the new international airport in the neighboring town of Bentonville.

The airport was nearing completion and I had to guard it at night against any and all trespassers. I quickly seized the assignment because I had always loved the night shift; it's so quiet and peaceful, it really gives you a lot of time to just sit back and think. I was told, however, that I could not drive on the runway. I never did, but on occasion I would pull my vehicle over to the side of the dirt road and would walk down the runway just for the fun of it.

On one particular evening I drove into the construction sight just as the construction workers were leaving and made my way to the empty terminal building to do my first rounds and make sure that all of the doors were locked and everybody had gone home for the night.

I happened upon five Wal-Mart executives that were still taking a tour of the building. They were extremely impressed with the progress and eyed everything over in wonder as two building contractors led them from area to area and room to room.

The seven men asked if I wanted to finish the tour with them. I probably shouldn't have because I would have been disobeying strict rules from my boss, but I jumped at the chance. Each man introduced themselves (I will not say their names here) and I introduced myself. We proceeded throughout the rest of the site for several more minutes and after the tour I escorted the men to the front gates where they got into their cars and abruptly left. Only one of the men I would ever see again.

The following night I arrived at work on time, and again made my way to the empty terminal building. I saw one of the Wal-Mart executives from the night before talking to three construction workers before they went home. I figured that I should check in with someone and slowly approached the group. I believe they were discussing cars. I awkwardly, but patiently, stood there waiting to make my presence known until the construction workers finished what they were saying and walked away.

The Wal-Mart executive then noticed me, thanked me for coming, and reintroduced himself. I will call him "Informant Smith" because he has asked that I keep his identity a secret. He walked me back to my patrol car and we got to talking. He told me how the control tower had been built too low and how they would go about raising it so that it would meet safety codes.

Smith and I really hit it off. I would meet him only three more times in the evenings before work started, and each time he and I would sit and talk for a good thirty to forty five minutes.

Thee years later, in May of 2001, I found myself living in Utah and working for Wal-Mart. I had worked for Wal-Mart Warehouse #4 many years ago from 1993 to1996, but now it was the 21st century and I had moved to Utah to attend Snow college in Ephraim, Utah. Later I got myself a job at Auto Meter Products, Inc. building battery testers. It lasted about a year and a half and I soon quit because of all the bureaucracy from within the company.

Jobs were very scarce in Sanpete County, and even though the county commission had tried their best to keep all businesses out, the only one to weasel their way in was none other than Wal-Mart. At the time I didn't care and quickly turned in my application. I was hired within two weeks because they needed night security and I had experience.

My job was to build grills and lawn mowers outside in front of the store, while keeping an eye on the parking lot and walking around the store every hour on the hour. I still loved night work, but now I was up to seven dollars and five cents an hour.

By 2004 I had worked at Wal-Mart for three years and had to ask myself why? If I had wanted to work for Wal-Mart I should have stayed in Rogers and Bentonville. That is where the home offices are located and several Supercenters and Neighborhood markets line the streets. Decisions that we make in life are very strange at times. And the strangest time of my life was about to come.

In late 2003 I had a run in with the lady from the claims department. I will call her "Tina." Her job was to file damage claims and get money back for damaged merchandise that was sent to the store from the manufacturer. I really liked her, she was the nicest person you'd ever want to meet and I would gladly help her out in any way that I could, until one morning around 6:00 a.m. when she called me over to her department to help her lift a computer that was too heavy for her. I quickly obliged. Fifteen minutes later she quickly turned into a screaming, raging lunatic when she had found out that I had not filled out a defective slip (A tiny slip of paper that lists the reason the merchandise is damaged).

Several witnesses, including an assistant manager and the personnel director, were in shock and later confided that she had two different personalities—good and evil.

She screamed that I had to fill out defective slips, it was store policy! She then began waving the policy in my face. I took it and told her to calm down. After hearing that she threatened to "deck me." The assistant manager escorted me out of the back room and told me to go home, then escorted her into the manager's office. I don't know if any action was taken against her behavior but I decided to talk to the store manager.

The meeting with the store manager was completely useless because he had only been on the job for one week and was still trying to get to know every one and get on their good side. So I had no choice but to call the district manager. He told me that her actions were unacceptable and, in truth, I was completely content with his response even if no action was taken, simply because, for the next several weeks after the incident she went on threatening several more people and assistant managers (So I wasn't her only victim). The only difference between yelling at me and yelling at the assistant managers was that she baked them peanut butter cookies as a bribe to keep her job.

Upon reading the store policy concerning defective slips, I found it very poorly written and very confusing. It states simply that "Associates," as we employees are called, should but do not have to fill out defective slips. It goes on to say that it is "your" responsibility. This is very confusing because the person at the home office in Bentonville who had written the policy had written it *to* the claims associate and to no one else.

To clarify this better I will print an excerpt from that policy:

> General Procedures, CG 202, Defective Slips.
> " . . . *If* an Associate finds defective merchandise in the store, that associate *should* fill out a defective slip, attach it to the merchandise, and take it to the Claims area.
> Although defective slips are *usually* filled out by someone other than the Claims Associate, it is *your* responsibility to ensure that each item has one . . ."

It was very confusing so I wrote a couple of letters to the home office to inform them that their policy was haphazardly written and was causing a lot of contention at our store. I never received a response.

I then waited a couple of weeks and tried to call them and was transferred from department to department. Nobody even knew what a defective slip was.

In my continuing game of phone tag I came across none other

than Informant Smith. I was so surprised and glad to hear him. I explained my situation and he, like every one else could not help me. He told me to call my district manager again—I never did. I let the situation drop. But I kept in touch with Smith and told him that I was now a writer and had written two science fiction novels and an off-the-wall comedy. He was very impressed and then brought me up to speed on what was going on in his life.

On one occasion when I called him, he seemed very upset. His mood had changed for the worse. He informed me of what had been going on at the home offices and then explained a few other things that were happening within the company.

I was shocked.

With his permission, and on the condition that I not reveal his name or anything else about his life, I asked if I could write everything that he told me into a book. He reluctantly agreed and so I wrote down all of the facts that he could reveal.

Smith has put in many, many years with Wal-Mart and wishes to retire with the company. I and everyone else must respect that.

Also included in this book is a brief history of Wal-Mart and it's founder Sam Walton for historical purposes only. Everything else was written down as dictated to me by "Informant Smith."

—Grant Lee

Chapter One

THE CONSPIRACY

How does Wal-mart continue to grow at an astonishing rate when most small stores, known as "Mom and Pop" stores, usually fail within the first two years? Is it because Wal-Mart sells the same merchandise but at a lower price? Maybe. Is it because the founder, Mr. Samuel Moore Walton is a real go getter? Perhaps. But the real reason is simply because of Wal-Mart's ties to the government.

Sam Walton's first big break came when he married his wife, Miss Helen Alice Robson, on Valentine's day in 1943. She was the daughter of a banker, and this gave Sam enough money and clout to bribe store owners in Siloam Springs and Bentonville, Arkansas, to sell their stores even though they had refused the offer time and time again. The pressure was great from Sam, with the help of his father-in-law, but Sam could persuade you with a smile and his laid back country charm, and soon the two widows from Kansas City gave in and sold their store in Bentonville to Sam for $20,000 (He purchased the store in Siloam Springs several years later).

As soon as Sam Walton took control of his new store and renovated it by knocking out a wall and combining it with a barbershop next door to make his store larger, he set out to make friends with the local politicians. Sam reasoned that he would need their friendship because the people of the community looked up to them; he also knew that they didn't earn their money but took it by force through taxes. Whether the economy was good or bad the government still made money. What better friends to have?

But even this was no small task. He started off making friends with the mayor and city council of Bentonville by taking them hunting or just sitting and talking on the front porch while sipping lemonade on a lazy Saturday afternoon. Later he would set his friendship in stone by donating generously to their campaign with steep contributions.

His strategy paid off slowly but surely and soon the local government was helping him out financially when ever they could. As Sam's company grew state wide, he was making friends with the Governor using the same method—Hunting, lemonade and contributions. When his company was well known nationally, again he used the same method—Hunting, lemonade and contributions.

Donating to their campaign definitely pushed Mr. Walton forward a few steps, but more than anything, it put him in the right place at the right time to be part of a national scheme by the federal government that would reimburse him one billion fold; it is a scam that will make other Wal-Mart scandals like the child sweat shops in Saipan and the false advertising that stated all products they sold were "Made in America" seem trivial by comparison, but I will discuss more about that later.

As for the city and state level, Mr. Sam was now a hometown hero, and since politicians could spend their campaign and contribution money anyway they pleased, they gladly used it to help Mr. Walton anyway they could, thus influencing his hundreds, if not thousands, of employees for guaranteed votes.

You scratch my back, I'll scratch yours.

The trick, however, was that Sam would have to meet the certain politician in person, face to face, and invite him or her to go hunting or have dinner with the family. He didn't just stick a check in the mail. He had to work very, very hard.

Proof of the final result concerning Wal-Mart/Government occurred on Friday, November 6, 1998 when President Bill Clinton flew into Highfill, Arkansas to dedicate a brand new, $70 million, international and cargo airport that was conveniently located just outside of Bentonville.

Air Force One arrived late on that somewhat cool, sunny afternoon, but not as late as everyone had predicted. The massive blue and white plane landed smoothly and taxied to a designated spot on the tarmac behind the stage where the dedication ceremonies would take place. President Clinton appeared within minutes and soon took his place on a decorated podium.

The audience, with an estimated attendance between 10,000 and 15,000 people, had been waiting for as long as six hours to catch a glimpse of the president. They were forced to stand behind metal barriers on the tarmac while state dignitaries, Wal-Mart executives and other VIPS were allowed into a roped off section beneath the stage where they could sit comfortably in chairs. The whole area was also blocked off from the rest of the airport by Wal-Mart semi trailers, which clearly pointed out who was the dominate figure at the proceedings.

Alice Walton, Sam Walton's daughter, was given a special gift that was wrapped in gold paper with a large red ribbon as a thank you for Wal-Mart's generous financial gift to the airport. She accepted the gift without saying a word.

President Clinton then reminisced about his northwest Arkansas past. He told the assembled crowd that as the plane came to a stop, he shared with Secret Service agents his excitement at returning to a familiar part of the state. "I told them," he said, "I want you to know this is where I started my political career. This is where I became familiar with the then-less developed part of northwest Arkansas and that one day this would be the site of a new airport. I have learned a lot in this area, including the location of a small community near Highfill during my less-than-successful bid for Congress in 1974. You know, I got tickled [before speaking]. I thought to myself, I wonder if I'm the only president who knows how to get to Hiwasse. I learned most of what I know going around on those back roads . . .

Over the years, numerous people have dedicated themselves to the idea of an airport, and those people deserve all the credit for the creation of this facility. They did all the work. Their efforts will be rewarded by even more growth and opportunity for northwest Arkansas in future generations, as easier transportation into and out of northwest Arkansas makes it easier for the area to share its abundance with the rest of the world, and as the area itself benefits from the sharing . . .

Our independence and our power depends on our interdependence."

Other excerpts from the dedication of XNA and President Clinton's speech can be found in: The Benton County Daily Record and The Morning News of Northwest Arkansas (11-7-98).

One has to ask why Mr. Clinton was driving around on the back roads of northwest Arkansas to win a state wide governor election or a nation wide congressional election anyway. Was he just in touch with the local hillbillies? I don't think so. Was it because Hillary Clinton served for eight years on Wal-Mart's board of directors? Absolutely! There was far more going on between the government and Wal-Mart than met the eye.

Many presidents would travel to northwest Arkansas to meet with Mr. Sam Walton but none more frequently than George Herbert Walker Bush and William Jefferson Clinton. In fact, on every visit that Bill Clinton would make to the Bentonville region he would always stop and have dinner at the AQ (Arkansas Quality) Chicken House, located in nearby Springdale, Arkansas.

When the president would make a special trip to Arkansas he would be escorted secretly, and of course first class, aboard the Marine One helicopter or Wal-Mart's private airline, the Eagle Express. Now, with the new airport, they can fly openly on Air Force One and nobody would think twice about it.

The reason for the frequent visits to Bentonville would be the most shocking and surprising secret that Informant Smith would ever entrust to me! A conspiracy that has gone on for thirty years and has gotten worse with President Bush, Clinton and George W. Bush.

If you are now prepared to hear about the scam, read on:

It is called "Operation Rollback." And considering the word *rollback* is used as Wal-Mart's signature phrase, to me, is like committing a crime in broad daylight and hiding in plain sight. It is just plain wrong.

Operation Rollback was an official agreement that Mr. Sam Walton himself and President Richard M. Nixon agreed to in August of 1973, under the direction of the U.S. Treasury and the United

States Mint (Copies of the signed contract are kept in a vault at the Wal-Mart Home Offices and in Washington DC).

The agreement refers to the fact that the government earns more money than is actually in print. For example, if the U.S. Mint prints a one dollar bill and that bill is placed into circulation, the person who receives that bill and spends it on, let's say a candy bar, will pay between five to seven cents in sales tax. In the State of Utah sales tax is 6.25 %, witch comes to about six cents per dollar, so I will use that as a further example.

As that dollar bill continues to circulate to seventeen people, at six cents, the government has just made one dollar. As the bill is circulated to thirty four people, the government has just made two dollars. And given that a dollar bill's life span is an estimated six years, and assuming one thousand people a year spend that single dollar for a total of six thousand people. The government has just made $375.00 on just a one dollar bill! Just imagine the millions and millions of dollars that are being printed and how much money the government is actually making!

This is where Operation Rollback comes in. The government rolls the extra money back to Wal-Mart to "fix" the numbers so that it appears that everything comes out even. This in turn keeps Wal-Mart in business and ahead of the game, and generates more votes for politicians because there are giant Wal-Mart stores everywhere and brand new airports, which gives the illusion that there is prosperity in the land so they can get more votes and get re-elected.

Again, if you scratch my back then I'll scratch yours.

Sales tax, of course, is a state tax and is designed to benefit each individual state but the federal government oversees the excess and makes sure that it is rolled back to big business. And since Wal-Mart is in good with the state and national government, it is first to receive the funds.

It is common knowledge, according to news reports, that even though all of the major airlines have filed for bankruptcy they are still in business thanks to the federal government that have bailed them out. This also goes for Worldcom and Enron; they too have received financial aid to stay in business—a kind gift that small local stores just don't receive.

To better illustrate the scam, let's assume that I shop at Mom and Pop's store and purchase a lollipop for one dollar plus tax. I pay in cash, and in turn, Mom and Pop's pay the tax to the government in the form of a check. The government will then take the excess amount after one dollar has been earned and gives that money (Also in the form of a check) to Wal-Mart who uses it specifically for growth, because who gets the money in exchange for land to build on? The city, county or state government. And whether or not any actual money has exchanged hands, the check given to the state is still good with the federal government.

In fact, President Nixon authorized the total amount of $1.3 million to be awarded to Wal-Mart each year specifically for "growth" nation wide. President George Bush Sr. brought the total sum up to $2.1 billion in 1990, and President Clinton nearly doubled that amount to a whopping $3.9 billion in 1995.

It is not known whether any other president has raised the dollar amount that Wal-Mart has received.

But President Nixon, at the time, was in a serious fix. He was right in the middle of the Watergate scandal and probably already knew his chances of being impeached were very likely. So, in 1973, almost one year to the day that Wal-Mart opened up their stock on the New York Stock Exchange in August of 1972, President Nixon quickly signed the Rollback plan, ensuring that he would receive four hundred and fifty shares of Wal-Mart stock, under an assumed name, that was guaranteed to succeed and bring in revenue for he and his family after his resignation in 1974 (Today one hundred shares of WMT original stock from 1972 is worth $20 million dollars).

He didn't just want to write himself a check with the extra money that each state received because it was simply too obvious. People would ask where was this money coming from? So by rolling it over to Wal-Mart and other big businesses in exchange for pure-profit stock, the numbers could remain hidden.

As Wal-Mart grew from the scam they would spend a considerable amount of money to the manufacturers (It certainly wasn't going to the associates) who would then build the products that Wal-Mart had ordered. The manufacturers would then pay taxes on virtually everything so they themselves could stay in business—thus, more money was going back to the government. What goes around comes around.

The tricky part of this little scheme was that a large portion of the Rollback money was being dispensed by Congressman Bud Shuster (R., Pa.). He was the House Committee chairman for Transportation and Infrastructure and directed billions of dollars directly to Wal-Mart, more than likely, through subtle grants and loans for the airport, various planes, and Wal-Mart's private trucking fleet.

Mr. Shuster had been in office since 1973 and so far has never had a close call in the polls. He travels lavishly around the country asking local chambers of commerce about their infrastructure needs, and many are more than happy to shell out taxpayer's hard earned money: For the 1998 election he raised $1.5 million in campaign contributions and spent $2,500 on campaign ads, then blew most of the rest on luxury hotels, ritzy restaurants, private jets and limousines.

Also in 1998, Shuster assembled a highway bill that authorized $217 billion dollars in new spending over six years. As the vote approached, he tried to sweeten the deal by bribing other members of Congress to see things his way by offering them $5 million to $10 million a piece for district needs. Rep. Tom Coburn (R., Okla.) called the offer a "vote buying scheme" and opposed the bill. However, Rep. Robert Ney (R., Ohio) got Shuster to invest $30 million around his district, including $40,000 for five toilets at a rest stop in Monroe County.

Yes, the federal government is indeed smooth. They have covered up so well that finding the extra money is next to impossible because it's no longer in their possession. As long as the money continues to float from one person to the next, the government will continue to make a profit, then roll it over to Wal-Mart to keep the scam going. This is one reason the government has been harassing Bill Gates and Microsoft. Microsoft hoards the billions of dollars that it has earned and has stopped a lot of the circulation. Perhaps it is more about Bill Gates harassing the government.

We have to remember this isn't a case of pulling a quarter out of an empty pocket, this a case about putting a quarter into an empty pocket and having it disappear. I am indeed paying sales tax and so are you and so is the next guy—it is all about numbers and credit. We really don't use cash anymore, we can actually go for a long time without ever seeing actual greenbacks since we use checks and credit cards so much of the time. This makes any kind of scam very hard to detect.

This example of extra tax numbers doesn't even include income tax and every other kind of tax. The government gets you coming and going!

But many people are probably thinking how can Republicans and Democrats both be in on this giant scam? They are completely different, right?

Wrong.

Lee Scott, the current president and CEO of Wal-Mart, said it best at a private meeting at the home office: " . . . there are absolutely no differences between Republicans and Democrats. They certainly have different views—completely different. But what are they viewing? They both are viewing bigger and better government!"

Mr. Scott is completely right. Republicans and Democrats want more power for the government, which means less freedom for the people, except for the choice of which coffee maker or blender to purchase at Wal-Mart.

The obvious connections that Republicans had with Wal-Mart became apparent on March 17, 1992 when President Bush awarded Sam Walton the Medal of Freedom, the highest honor that a civilian can receive. Now I'm not saying that Mr. Sam didn't earn the award but 1992 just happened to be an election year and President Bush was trying to win a second term against none other than Bill Clinton who just happened to be from Arkansas. Mr. Bush figured that if he could take that central state and knock Clinton out of the picture he might have a chance at winning the election—but it was not to be. He lost out to Clinton who did go on to serve two consecutive terms simply because he had closer ties to Wal-Mart.

Sam Walton passed away almost a month later on April 5, 1992. If the Republicans had to brag about their connections with Wal-Mart, awarding Sam with the medal in 1990 or 1991 would have been a little more appropriate.

*   *   *

We must remember that the government works for the people,

that is why they are called "public servants." Public meaning: The
people as a whole. And servant meaning: To be subordinate or
subservient to; to act in an inferior or secondary part.

We constantly confuse our boss at work or our priest or bishop
at church with elected politicians. Our boss at the office can tell us
what to do because they either own the place or are authorized by
the owner to tell us what to do; the same rule applies for church,
they can tell us what to do because they either own the building or
are authorized by the owner to excommunicate us, or not. But
elected officials are hired by us through the process of voting, and
so they must obey the majority! If they just go into office and do
whatever they want to do they are not doing their job.

Mayors can decide small things on their own like whether or
not the city building needs a new phone line, the public shouldn't
have to worry about that, but if someone wants to build a high-rise
tower right in the middle of town, it is the mayor's responsibility to
do what the majority wants. If the majority of people want a tower
in town, it is the mayor's duty to get one, if the majority of people
say no, it is the mayor and city council's job to listen and turn the
offer down. If the elected officials do not do this they should be
fired and replaced in the next election.

We are very blessed in this country. We don't need to have a
rebellion or a violent revolution; we don't need to storm the White
House with guns blazing. All we need to do is vote! We need to stop
re-electing the same idiots right back into office and put people in
that are willing to serve by listening.

Remember, we have many other political parties to choose from
other than just Republicans and Democrats. There is the Libertarian
party; the Constitution party; the American party; the Independence
party; the Reform party; the Prohibition party; the Natural Law party;
the Green party if you are an environmentalist, and many, many
others.

But I do have to give the citizens credit, if it were up to them
Wal-Mart would not be as big as it is today, the blame lies mostly with
the city officials and the many little tricks of the trade that the
government has.

A couple of years ago I was working for a company called Western
Watts Inc. located in Ephraim, Utah. It was a small business that

would conduct political phone surveys all over the nation, but we weren't allowed to say where we were calling from. All we could tell the person that answered the phone was that we were calling from the inter-mountain west. "Where the heck is that?" they would say. We kept our mouth shut, hoping that they would assume we were calling from right down the street. But the fact was we weren't, we were over half way across the nation, and to make matters worse, we didn't even know which candidate or politician we were conducting the surveys for, all we were told was that it was a Republican. Each interview had a different name for the company. For example, I remember calling Washington D.C. and saying that I was with Potomac Survey Research and was calling about local impact laws. One question was worded like this: "If local taxes have to be raised to fund needed transportation priorities, which is the fairest way? Raise the local gas tax? Raise the local sales tax? Or raise the local income tax?"

Notice how many times the word "local" is used? But it sounds like a reasonable question doesn't it? No. Because there were two other possible answers that we were not allow to read out loud: "Do not raise taxes," and "I don't know." We could only mark those answers if the person at the other end chose to say that. But if the person that we were interviewing said such things as: "I hate taxes!" or "The government can take those taxes and . . ." We still weren't allowed to mark those answers on the grounds of being biased unless the interviewee said word for word: "Do not raise taxes."

Needless to say, after being promoted to a supervisor, I quit after a week and a half.

The government, as we know it today, does have its down side and so does Wal-Mart. We must remember that Wal-Mart is not a hometown store—it is big business whose founder just happens to come from a small town.

Wal-Mart is corrupt. Each individual store makes money by selling every day stuff, the overall company makes money from stock prices and the Rollback scam. That is why growth is so important, they absolutely need growth to keep stock prices high and flourishing. There are many other things wrong with Wal-Mart but who's going to accuse them of anything when the first thing that you see when you walk in their front doors is a nice old man or woman kindly greeting you.

Wal-Mart has said that they will leave town if they are not wanted there, but they will decide that after the store has opened. I wish that we could vote them out like we can with politicians.

Chapter Two

ODD-PRICE SALE

What is an odd-price sale? It is an optical illusion that every store in the nation, and possibly the world, uses in its pricing to make merchandise appear to cost less by marking it down one penny, a nickel, or a dime so that the end result comes out to be $8.99 or $7.95. The effect works because we in America read from left to right and tend to be a bit lazy. As we dash into the store to make a purchase, we look up at the sign and get about as far as the first number. "Oh, it's only eight dollars and something cents," we think to ourselves. We constantly forget to add on the sales tax which brings our purchase to over nine dollars. And let's not forget about the "Gotchas." We dash to the rear of the store where they have conveniently placed the milk—which is a necessity—and on our way out we pass the display of cookies. "That will go great with milk," we think to ourselves again. Now we've purchased cookies and milk which is not exactly healthy *and* has now cost us a small fortune.

Gotcha!

But Wal-Mart takes great pride in the odd-price sale. In fact, that is the whole basis for its current ad campaign on television. We see a smiley face flying around the store and lowering the price of their merchandise by a few more pennies while several associates stand around and smile contentedly. This is a very, very subtle rip off—and the worst part is that it's made to appear friendly. Don't be fooled. The odd-price sale accounts for billions of dollars in sales each year that Wal-Mart proudly brags about. It is money that you could have saved. Remember that—Always.

The odd-price sale started out simple enough: It originated in 1875 by Melville Stone, the owner of the Chicago Daily News. He sold copies of his newspaper for only a penny but when business dropped and he looked into why, he discovered that there weren't enough pennies in circulation. So Stone traveled to the United States Mint in Philadelphia and brought back barrels of pennies to Chicago. The problem then became how to get the pennies back into circulation. Stone ended up persuading local merchants to sponsor "odd-price sales," during which they would sell their merchandise for a penny under the regular price. The scheme did the trick! People had pennies again, and Stone's paper flourished.

Stores still use it today, but not in such an honest mode. Wal-Mart is by far the worst of the bunch.

If you find yourself shopping at Wal-Mart and want to save yourself some real money, remember to only buy what you need, never shop while you are hungry and get out of the store as fast as you can. The longer you stay the more likely you are to buy something. These practices are just plain common sense but if you want to save even more money I would also highly recommend not shopping at Wal-Mart in the first place. If you are looking for car parts or car accessories then go to an auto parts store where you can get quality parts with expert advice and not have to worry about being totally lost and uninformed, and then leaving the store with a shopping cart full of other useless junk that you never intended to buy. Wal-Mart sells generic parts, like spark plugs, that can be used on half a dozen other vehicles, the price may be cheaper but the life of these parts will only be one third as long, and after you have purchased that action figure that your son just noticed and begged you for, you may end up spending more money than you should have.

Another poor item that Wal-Mart sells is the vacuum cleaner. The ones they offer at Wal-Mart are low, low quality and don't suck up directly into the bag, they suck the dirt up through the hose which is placed off to the side down by the brush. The vacuum then sends the dirt up through the hose and then down into the bag. You only pick up one-tenth of the dirt, and if something happens to the hose, you don't clean anything at all. Purchase your vacuums at a specialized vacuum shop.

But real savings at Wal-Mart comes on all clearance and holiday merchandise that didn't sell during the original season. For example, one customer came into the store in late January and found two, eight feet tall, inflatable snowmen that were selling before Christmas for $29.95 ($30.00). They had been misplaced on the wrong aisle and were purchased for $1.50 each after the Christmas clearance sale had ended. This *only* happens on misplaced clearance and holiday merchandise. Department managers are only allowed to mark post-holiday merchandise down by 20 to 30%, depending on how many clearance dollars they are allowed by the company. But if this merchandise were to turn up two or three months after all other clearance items are sold out, the savings are incredible. The extra discount won't work if an item turns up on aisle four and similar items have already been marked down to a steady clearance price on aisle three. Every item on clearance *has* to be completely out of stock for a week or two. Most holiday and clearance items after that aren't reordered again for another year.

Clearance items are marked with a red price sticker directly on the merchandise and are located under a bright yellow sign with red letters.

Wal-Mart also has a policy that the costumer is always right. If the customer argues that a price was marked lower than it actually was then Wal-Mart has to sell it to them at that price. Associates may argue it with you or send someone to check the listed price, but if the customer keeps insisting, they *must* sell it to the customer at the lower price. This also works with two items that are bound together, if the customer thinks that it was supposed to be sold as one item, they can get two for the price of one.

Those are just a couple of ways that people can save money at Wal-Mart, but if you keep returning to Wal-Mart hoping to find new bargains and new merchandise from new companies every time, it won't work. Yes, Wal-Mart sells a lot of stuff. It accounts for sixty five percent of all landfill space in America, but Wal-Mart only sells merchandise from a few selected manufactures. No other seller really has a chance, even if their product costs less and performs better.

Every six months, each department at Wal-Mart sets a new mod. (Module); this means that they will move every item on any given aisle around to make it appear that new items have come in, or stirs things up so that stuff that wasn't selling very well before can now have a different location and possibly be seen a little better by the customer. At times, brand new merchandise does come in, but it is only new products from the same old companies. Wal-Mart also requires manufacturers to repackage old merchandise to keep things looking fresh.

Sellers of new products must talk directly to the home offices in Bentonville. Trying to sell products to local stores won't work unless you have a one hundred thousand dollar insurance policy, just in case your product falls down on some poor child's head, but even if you had the policy, merchandise still has to be authorized by the home offices.

If a vendor has courage enough to travel to Bentonville to sell his or her goods, prepare for a run-around! Sellers will be scheduled, ushered into the home offices like cattle, and sat in a large room full of cheap metal folding chairs that are designed to give the impression that Wal-Mart is poor. And if that isn't bad enough, 95% of the vendors are rejected before they walk through the front doors.

Wal-Mart only supports a very, very few selected manufacturers and sellers. So in essence, every store sells exactly the same thing; smaller stores might sell less because they have less space, but all merchandise is the same. The only difference is, every department might be located in a different part of the store. For example, If you were to find colored baskets in the crafts department that you liked, they might be located on the top shelf sitting next to each other in a certain order, yellow on the far left, pink in the middle, and blue on the right. If you then traveled to another Wal-Mart, you would find the same baskets in the same order on the top shelf, yellow, pink and blue. The aisles might run different directions; the first store's aisles might run east and west and the second store's aisles might run north and south, but you will find the exact same items in the exact same place.

This is because *everything* is controlled by the home office. *Every* mod. must be set up the same way. This is to maintain order but also gives Wal-Mart the advantage over smaller stores. Mom and Pop's have to worry about buying the right merchandise and figure out if it will sell or not. They also have to worry about advertising; they have to worry about placing each item in the right place in the store; they have to worry about payroll; they even have to worry about how to get the money to open their store in the first place, so forth and so on. But the local Wal-Mart next door only has to worry about two things: selling and how to do it with a smile. Every item that comes in is sent by the home office and each store receives the merchandise whether they need it or not. They don't have to worry about receiving the money to open the store; they don't have to worry about where to place the merchandise; the advertising is done for them; payroll is done for them—*everything* is done for them! What a life, huh?

But the main reason that Wal-Mart has tried to get rid of the private vendors and have the Frito Lay, Hostess and Little Debbie baking companies deliver directly to the warehouses, is to eliminate the middle man and save Wal-Mart money so that they can show their power. So far, with these three companies, it has failed, and good for them!

The vendors are the main life source for Mom and Pop's and end up costing the smaller stores additional fees that they just can't afford if they want to continue competing with Wal-Mart. So Wal-Mart had a plan; they would open a chain of Sam's Clubs all around the nation where small stores and other businesses can buy merchandise from them and eliminate the middle man, but the thing is, vendors can also buy merchandise from them, which didn't accomplish anything other than Wal-Mart has weaseled its way into the big picture. Before, you had manufactures selling to vendors, who sold to small stores; now you have manufactures selling to Wal-Mart, who sells to vendors, who sells to small stores. This ends up costing Mom and Pop stores and the community far more in the long run.

Another reason that Wal-Mart opens in a small town is that the smaller stores just can't compete, Wal-Mart's Comp. Shoppers (Comparative Shoppers) see to that by writing down every bargain price of the surrounding stores and beating their price by using odd-price sales or other methods. In fact, there are three main reasons why Wal-Mart opens in small towns that have a population of three thousand people or less.

1. Small stores can't compete and if they do it's nothing to worry about.
2. There is nothing else for young people to do in small towns except to hang out at Wal-Mart.
3. Opening in a small town gives the "hometown" appearance that the company needs to compete in the global market.

Now, let me take you inside a Wal-Mart and explain how things are done.

When you walk into a store the first thing that you enter is the vestibule. This is a decompression zone that allows you relax from the hustle and bustle of the parking lot. This works almost instantaneously, and with the friendly smile from the kindly, old door greeter, the effect is that much more enhanced.

As you enter the store itself you are overwhelmed by the smell of baking bread or the sight of fresh produce, depending on the store. This gives the store a clean, hometown style that makes you want to relax and stay longer. That is where they've got you! The longer you stay, the more money you will spend, and with a McDonald's, Radio Grill restaurant or a snack bar located somewhere inside, you are sure to stay and spend more.

Customers will always walk through the door and head to the right, so Wal-Mart has set up a series of displays to draw the customer further into the store one display at a time in a circular pattern so that every inch of the store has a draw (popular selling merchandise). And since people naturally walk forward instead of side to side, most signs are hung perpendicular to the customer instead of parallel.

Benches are also strategically placed around the store for the family of customers that need a rest or for the husband that is waiting for his wife to finish shopping. They are also placed in various locations for girls that shop in groups or to create an atmosphere of relaxation. Without these benches most customers will invent places to sit and most can be hazardous. But seating areas or chairs are key! They are there to slow the customer down and get them to stay longer. Again this is to get you to buy more.

Also at the end of every aisle are shelves that are called "End Caps." These shelves feature special merchandise that isn't necessarily on sale. This is one aspect of the store that the home offices don't control because end caps feature merchandise that each individual store has too much of. For example, if too many microwaves are ordered or are automatically sent by the home offices, each store will place them on an end cap. The rule is that they must fill the entire end cap and feature only one item, or also include similar microwaves that are listed for the exact same price. It is against the rules to feature five microwaves for fifty dollars along side eight blenders for twenty dollars, but some stores do cheat. Some will feature a hundred different clearance items at a hundred different prices—this ends up looking like clutter, but most stores do it anyway.

Other features are "Four-Ways" and "Dump Bins." Four-ways are shelves that sit in the middle of the main action alley (The larger aisles where most of the traffic flows) and will feature four different products at four different prices; the same almost goes for dump bins. They sit in the middle of the action alley and come in two different sizes, short and tall. They allow the store to dump two different items down inside, such as basketballs or pillows. This merchandise is not on sale either—it is merely overstock ordered by the store. But there is a principle to the madness; items that sit back to back in a dump bin tend to sell better than just one item sitting in the bin alone. I don't know how or why it works, but it works. People probably assume that it is on sale even though they can find it in it's home for the exact same price.

The "Home" is the designated spot on the shelf where any given item can be found in the store (The Mod.). For example, toasters are located in the Housewares Department on the appliance aisle on the left hand side near the bottom. That is their home. If you are looking for a particular toaster and it is not in its home, and you can't find it on a four-way or end cap, then you might try checking on the "Riser." The riser is the very top shelf and should have a thin, purple strip of paper fastened along the front that reads: "Ask for help with items on the top shelf." This is where most overstock is stored instead of being stashed away in the back room where nobody will ever find it. The rule that coincides with the risers in the store is that overstocked toasters should be placed in a four foot section above the home, but this doesn't always happen, sometimes it will be across the aisle or even two aisles down. Check these locations before confronting a store employee.

Play Station gaming systems are usually locked up behind glass, but I once found a couple on the riser which were accessible to anyone.

In a couple of locations in the store beneath the risers are "Cheater Shelves." They are regular sized shelves where smaller merchandise, such as the ones sold on pegs, can be temporarily stored until the home is empty. This too is overstock; so if your hand held can opener is out of stock, check this area before confronting an associate.

I tell you to check these areas first because if you ask a casual associate where something is, this is the first place that they will look simply because, a lot of times, they don't have any idea where it is either. If you still can't locate an item that you want to buy then ask specifically for a department manager. They will scan the price tag of the empty home on a hand held computer called a Telxon. This will tell the department manager everything about the item, like how many are in stock; how many are coming in, or *if* anymore are coming in. These are very useful little computers; they work by remote from the stores main computer and can access all needed information through the SMART system.

Another thing that I should mention now, is that if you locate a piece of merchandise that you want to buy and there are two yellow price labels (They will be red if it's on clearance) underneath the item, the accurate one will be, more often than not, located to the left. That is how we were told to stock merchandise—place each object to the right of the price point.

If you find a loose piece of merchandise, like a flyswatter, and want to check the price by what you believe to be the empty home, you can check the UPC number (Bar code) and compare it to the small number *under* the listed price on the yellow tag that is located on the shelf. The UPC number will be to the right of the price in the grocery department.

The term "Plugging" is a word that is used to describe merchandise that is placed in the wrong home. "Stuffing" means that a piece of merchandise is too far to the right and is taking up space in another object's home. Wal-Mart has strange names and words for everything.

Now, the above information does come in handy, but let me tell you something that you really should know: Do not ask an associate to check the back room for out of stock merchandise, it won't do any good. Most merchandise in the back is shrink wrapped to pallets and placed on top of the outrigger (Thick metal shelving). No Associate is going to go through all of that stuff by hand looking for one object; the department manager, however, is your best bet. He or she can use the Telxon and tell you if the particular item is in the store, but they too aren't going to search through everything by hand. It will more than likely be worked out onto the sales floor within a day or two anyway through the 7-Day, 14-Day and 30-Day rule. This was a system set up by Wal-Mart to keep merchandise from piling up in the back room. Merchandise that is shipped directly from the warehouse should be out on the sales floor in seven days. Assembly products (Merchandise that the warehouse does not have in stock but will be receiving soon) should be out on the sales floor no later than fourteen days. And new mod (The new items from the old manufactures that come in every six months, which also includes speciality merchandise and holiday features), should be placed out on the sales floor no later than thirty days from the time that it arrives on the truck. Merchandise that is called "Tab," which falls under the thirty day rule, has been specifically ordered because it will appear in the next Wal-Mart advertisement, but when it does come out and is stocked on the shelves, customers have to look for the orange signs to find it.

Everything from the 7, and 14 day rule is kept in bins (Shelves that are built out of sections of the outrigger), but is nothing more than overstock. These products, again, will probably be found on the risers. If not, the department manager is supposed to work that freight out onto the sales floor long before seven, fourteen and thirty days has expired, but this doesn't always happen because of other problems that might occur.

If you insist that an associate check the back room, various departments do have overstock bins in the back room where some merchandise is accessible, but like everything else, they try to work that out onto the sales floor as soon as possible. Plus, your product may or may not even be there.

Asking a department manager for help in books and electronics is also useless because these departments only order the top ten or top one hundred best sellers. If it's not in, it's not in. If it comes in—great! Wonderful! They will just go look on the shelf like every one else.

But if you've had your eye on that coveted barbeque grill, the one you've been waiting for your entire life, which happens to be completely out of stock, and it can't be located anywhere else in the store, it will probably be shipped in within a day or two. Wal-Mart has scanners at every checkout stand in the front of the store that will automatically re-order an item once it has been paid for. This system is called P.O.S. (Point of sale). It is a pretty handy feature but can sometimes cause a lot of problems and expense because the department managers can also order more of the same merchandise from the wharehouse.

I remember one incident when a customer purchased a plastic owl in the garden center. The owl was designed to scare pigeons and other birds away from your home or garden, but they didn't work and didn't sell very well. The scanners, of course, automatically re-ordered another case or two, and so did the department manager. Somehow, someone goofed on the numbers and we ended up receiving two cases of owls every night for a month. We had plastic owls coming out of our ears! We were still trying to sell those things in the middle of winter.

I don't know how anyone goofed on that one. Assistant managers are supposed to authorize every order placed by the department managers before they go through. You would think that the warehouse would say: "Whoa! Hold on a minute! Why do they need five hundred plastic owls?" But this kind of mistake happens all the time. I guess it's because they figure that we have quite a few end caps and four-ways to fill.

It just adds up to a lot of stuff that we as Americans just don't need—you know, junk. That is why the best selling item at Wal-Mart is the Sterilite and Rubbermaid plastic boxes. Because we buy piles and piles of useless junk at Wal-Mart then take it home and store it like pack rats. Why? Why do we do this? Why do assistant managers authorize purchases like Congress, the Senate and the Legislature by signing things that they don't read first. Who Knows?

Maybe it's because they have a thankless job. But most assistant managers that I know can end up working sixteen or seventeen hours a day simply because Wal-Mart owns them. They are paid a steady salary so Wal-Mart doesn't care how many hours they work. I've gone to work on the night shift around ten o' clock and my superiors have already been there since about nine. Long after I get off my shift at 6:30 a.m., they often stay and continue to work until 11 a.m. or 1 p.m., this is because they are hired to oversee the night crew *and* the I.C.S. (Inventory Control Specialist) team that work during the day.

That doesn't even include the fact that they are on call when they have a day or night off. They must wake up in the middle of the night and rush back to the store every time the alarm is set off, which happens constantly, and ninety nine percent of the time it is a false alarm.

I, myself, have set the alarm off on three different occasions: The first incident took place while I was working security at the store and the assistant manager at the time didn't completely lock the garden center door. I opened it in an attempt to get back into the building, not knowing he had attempted to lock it. Within seconds I had everyone inside covering their ears and buckling to their knees from the intense, ear piercing scream. The police arrived shortly and I explained everything. The second incident was after I had accidently set a pallet down too hard on the floor just inside the same door, setting off a motion detector. And the third, happened a year later as I was heading outside through, yes, the same door.

That door had it in for me.

Fortunately I never did get into severe trouble for setting off the alarm, but the exhausted assistant managers would stagger over to find out just why I had interrupted their sleep. I apologized profusely.

Let me take a minute to explain the different levels of management that Wal-Mart has at the individual stores: The lowest are the department managers, I talked about them earlier, and as their name implies, they are over each individual department. Slightly over them, though they don't often meet, are the support managers, they work mostly on the night shift. One will oversee the general merchandise side of the store and the other will oversee the grocery side. They have the power to tell the common associates what to do, but can only give verbal warnings for any wrong doing. The next level up the chain of command are the assistant managers; they are over everything and end up doing most of the supervising duties. If they see any wrong doing, they can issue a "Coaching," which is just a polite way of saying, "I'm writing you up."

And last, but certainly not least, are the store managers; they oversee the multitude of assistant managers that each store has and have the ability to fire anyone. Their main job is to be tall. The bigger they are the more likely they are to be appointed to this position. I know quite a few assistant managers that are far better qualified for this job but are left out simply because they don't have that domineering aura.

I believe that the role and job description of the assistant managers can best be described by using a dentist or doctor's office as an example. Close your eyes for a minute and picture yourself going into a doctor's office. You see the receptionist or nurse, they are the ones that have you fill out all of the paper work and then escort you down the hall, weigh you and take your blood pressure, then escort you into a small room and ask you what is wrong. After several minutes of waiting, the high and mighty doctor finally comes in, gives you his two cents worth, turns you back over to the nurse who administers most of the tests, then leads you back down the hall, takes your check and reschedules you for another appointment next month.

That is how it works. The doctor is a lot like the store manager— he's there but a lot of times you don't know why. Although, the store manager generally leads the Wal-Mart cheer, and many people know what that is! The legendary Wal-Mart cheer! Actually it should be called the "The Cheer" because all you are re really doing is spelling the name of the place. Many high schools use it to spell the name of their school: "Give me an 'R'! Give me an 'H'! Give me an 'S'! What's that stand for? 'Roger's High School! Rah!"

The Wal-Mart cheer is chanted exactly same way. You clap your hands in unison and shout: "Give me a 'W'! Give me an 'A'! Give me an 'L'! Give me a squiggly! (I don't know why they still use the squiggly since it hasn't been used in store signs for twenty years. They should change it to a star.) Give me an 'M'! Give me an 'A'! Give me an 'R'! Give me a 'T'!" . . . Now this is where things get complicated because over the years Wal-Mart has added a ton of additional material to the end of the cheer which now makes it go on for another hour and a half: "What's that spell? Wal-Mart! Who's number one? The customer! What store number are we? 1567! Are we safe workers? Yes! Are we going to take over the world? Yes! What are our top ten principles? Number one is . . ."

Well, okay, that might be a slight exaggeration, but you get the idea. They sing the glorious praises of Wal-Mart at every start-up meeting, which is another one of Wal-Mart's trademarks. The "Start-up Meeting" is a chance for every associate to get together before their shift and have an orientation of where the store stands on sales and other needed business. I personally like the idea of a start-up meeting because you feel like you are part of the team and have a say in what goes on, even if you don't. This sort of meeting would have come in handy with other jobs that I've had, especially in the manufacturing field when you stagger in to work first thing in the morning and drowsily get to your work station and try to set forth, unknowingly, to build and fill your orders. A start-up meeting first thing in the morning would give employees a definite chance to slowly wake up and find out what is going on.

When I worked for a company called Auto Meter Products, Inc., building battery testers and other components for high performance vehicles, you had to be at your work station at exactly 6:30 a.m. If you had just clocked in at exactly 6:30 you were considered late because you weren't working and ready to go. But the fact is, you weren't ready to go anyway until you found out what was going on by asking around or had been with the company long enough to automatically know through qualified experience.

Most companies are afraid that if they had a start-up meeting they would be accused of stealing from Wal-Mart, but believe me, Wal-Mart does not hide the fact that they stole the idea for the cheer and start-up meetings from other companies. In fact, they brag about it constantly! They stand there and proudly ramble on about how Sam had stolen other ideas from Ben Franklin and JC Penney stores in the early part of his career when he was employed by them and how they will carry on in that great tradition.

They probably stole the idea to pay low wages from other companies as well. I had to take a five cent an hour pay cut when I quit Auto Meter and started to work for Wal-Mart. I did it because I had never really been a morning person and was looking for an evening or night shift, and was extremely happy that I had found one. To be honest, I was glad to be out of the manufacturing industry altogether because of the extreme safety rules that OSHA had imposed. Don't get me wrong, Wal-Mart has more than its fair share of safety rules, but not as much as many companies that must build things for a living.

In my mind OSHA (Occupational Safety and Health Administration) should limit its power. I, of course, want to work in a safe environment but giving anyone the ability to make sure that things are done safely is not a good idea because it's a limitless power. The world is *not* safe and there are no end to the rules that you can come up with to make things a little safer. Much like lawyers who can sue for anything. They can sue for every single injustice until there is a rule against everything, then they can sue because we have too many rules. It probably won't end. And most of their suits end up becoming actual law if it makes its way up to the Supreme Court. Does this mean that lawyers and judges will end up running the country one day instead of elected officials? I don't know, simply because many of their law suits will probably end up ruling each other out. For example, a suit that allows a homosexual marriage to take place in one state will allow a similar marriage to take place in every state, but then that could allow for polygamy to be legal, and incest to be legal, and who knows what else could be legal. So, in the long run, are we gaining more freedoms or losing them?

I, myself, do not believe in polygamy for religious reasons, but also because polygamy leaves the ugly guy out. Think about it. If some hunk had two wives and the ugly guy had none, then some gorgeous blond bombshell comes along, she could easily choose the gentleman with the chiseled features and become the third wife, leaving the poor ugly sap out in the cold. Maybe that is why we have single marriages between two people, a man and a woman. Some homely king or president probably felt sorry for his unfortunate brothers.

But now getting back to the inner workings of Wal-Mart; the company only promotes from within. If you have been with the company for about a year or more, and are in good standing, you can enter into an internship and work your way to the position of an assistant manager. This is to ensure that you will do things Wal-Mart's way and not your own. Why would you do it any other way when you've done it their way for so long? You probably wouldn't and they're banking on it!

In fact, you are programed to follow Wal-Mart's path from the moment that you are hired. Each new associate must complete several hours of orientation consisting of lectures from assistant managers, watch several hours worth of instructional and informative videos, then perform four or more hours (forty to ninety minutes at a time) worth of C.B.L. (Computer Based Learning) programs.

C.B.L.s are video clips and short tests that are taken on computers. They consist of such things as: safety issues; how to work a forklift; how to fold towels; how to operate the trash compactor; how to work a cash register, etc. Every time that a new clip is produced by the home office, every associate must find time to take the test, no matter how long you've worked for the company.

Every new associate also receives a discount card that is good for ten percent off any general merchandise (G.M.) purchase. This card will not work on groceries and you can only allow family that you are living with, such as your wife or husband, to use the card. Friends, neighbors and other associates that want to borrow the card are out! But if you still live at home with mom and dad—they are in! Cashiers are not allowed to ring up sales for family members or friends, and no associate is allowed to take business cards from anyone.

These are just little tidbits about Wal-Mart that I thought were interesting, but one of the bigger secrets that Wal-Mart has is that they have to sell for less because they have no other choice. When men shop they get in and get out so Wal-Mart's appeal must fall to women and they don't accomplish this very well because women need privacy when they shop—they absolutely have to have it. When women shop for cosmetics, for example, they need space and a place where they can try them on in front of a mirror, analyze it, and try something else without other customers rushing by in busy, narrow aisles, and without anyone else gawking at them. In the dressing room area they need *time*, time to try one thing on, then another, and finally get their friend's opinion or advice. Wal-Mart offers none of this. They are just trying to get as many customers in as they can. The end. Period. So they have absolutely no choice but to lower the price as low as they can go to make up for the difference. Women can purchase the product because it's cheap, take it home and *then* try it on, if she doesn't like it she can bring it back and exchange it. Maybe she will even buy a toilet bowl brush or a box of garbage bags upon her return. Truly romantic!

This also applies to jewelry and everything else that is designed for women—and even if there are no other customers around, there is no privacy! They are watching you! If not through cameras then through any other means of security that is possible. Just because you walk through the front entrance and see a nice old lady doesn't mean that you are at grandma's house. Two girls that I used to work with were stocking cosmetics at 2:30 in the morning after the store was closed. When break time had been called over the intercom they sat down on the carpet next to the jewelry department to talk for awhile. The next day they were confronted because they had been seen on the security cameras and were told that all breaks and lunches had to be confined to the break room. They weren't in severe trouble but it goes to show that you are being watched every second of the day.

But don't be too paranoid, most security calls that are broadcast over the intercom are bogus. Calls that state: "We have a code such and such in the stationary department!" simply means that the associate in stationary is leaving for lunch or they are asking for an assistant manager to come and inspect the department for cleanliness and safety. I don't think this type of call is a very good idea because it is just too confusing. I was shopping in the produce section one day and the produce department manager came over the intercom and said that they had a code 15 in produce! I happened to be the only person in produce at the time and I know for a fact that I wasn't trying to steal apples by shoving them down my shirt, but I still felt guilty, which can ruin the shopping experience for most customers. Besides that, I don't see how that code will stop shoplifting. What if someone was just about to steal a CD over in electronics right at that moment? They probably could get away with it knowing full well that security was rushing over to produce to tackle someone for trying to make off with a kiwi.

Every other call for security might be accurate but the more important calls will be done by calling out a color. For example, code black is for bad weather; code red is for fire; code blue is for a bomb threat; code white is for an accident; code green is for a hostage situation; code orange is for a chemical spill; code Adam is for a missing child; code brown is for a shooting; code sunshine, or code yellow, is to stop what you are doing and help the nearest customer, and code H is to help the associate that just paged for help to lift something heavy. Most theft or other security issues, such as following customers, will be handled over the assistant manager's walkie-talkie radio.

And speaking of bright colors, let me say one final thing. Watch out for the flying smiley face! In all of my years of working for Wal-Mart I've never once had the opportunity to see the smiley face flying around diligently lowering prices. I think it's because Wal-Mart doesn't even own the smiley face; it is public domain and can be purchased by anybody. But by using the smiley face and other public domain characters such as Robin Hood or a construction worker, Wal-Mart can place a trademark on the cute little guy and somehow end up with both characters!

Chapter Three

INSIDE THE WAREHOUSE

A general Wal-Mart warehouse is as large as three or four football fields and appears relatively like a Sam's Club on the inside, with almost the same floors, walls and ceilings. The material that is used to make up all of the bins, shelves and storage units are made from the same steel outriggers used in the backrooms of all Wal-Mart retail stores. The steel is usually painted green, orange or sometimes blue.

When a shipment arrives from the manufacturer, either by their own truck or by UPS or FedEx, the shipment is quickly unloaded and re-stacked onto separate pallets throughout the receiving dock, or receiving bay. After everything is checked in and all paperwork is taken care of, an associate would come by with a small computer on a roller cart and approach every re-stacked pallet that has been shrink wrapped and neatly laid out between yellow lines that have been painted on the floor. The associate will then re-count every box on the pallet and confirm that it has been correctly entered into the computer. At that point she will print out an identity number, generally five numbers long, and stick it to the box that has been stacked on the top left hand corner.

After that entire process has been completed, a forklift operator will come by, pick up the pallet of merchandise and drive it to the appropriate storage area in the warehouse based on the number that is written on the sticker and place it in the designated outriggers until it is time to ship it to the stores.

The next stage in the operation is the order filling. Labels, approximately three inches by four inches, are printed up based on what every store in the district will need, or will get whether they need it or not. These labels are white with a giant bar code printed across the top two-thirds of the label itself. The bottom one-third contains all of the information that each piece of merchandise will need to get to the right store. It contains the store number, the date, a description of what the box of merchandise contains and even the department number it is supposed to go to when it reaches the store (Dept. 5 is electronics, Dept. 14 and 15 are housewares, etc.). Each label is also specially designed to have the middle section tear out so that store associates can move that section of the label and place it on the upper lefthand corner of the box when they place it in the backroom storage bins for the 7-Day, 14-Day and 30-Day rule. It's a nice way for the warehouse to help out the stores.

Throughout the warehouse are "Modules." These modules are three hundred to six hundred feet long and are four stories high. Modules are, again, made out of thin steel outriggers and look as though they might tip over at any minute.

The order-fillers, after arriving to work and attending their start up meeting, will put on their back belts, their small, two pocket tan aprons and their walkie-talkie radios and head for the first level of their designated module. One, or possibly two, people per module. They then arrive at the first station and sign out the labels for the first batch. Each "Batch," as they are called, will fill the orders for about ten to fifteen stores; batch 20, 21 and 22 are taken care of by the day shift, and batch 23, 24, 25, 26, 27 and 28 are taken care of by the night shift. 23-28 are much smaller orders, of course, but I'm not sure why the batch numbers only start and end in the twenties. Perhaps it's because other warehouses take care of the rest.

After the labels for batch 23 are signed out, the order-filler will go down the left side of the first level and take freight from each slot that is printed on the bottom left hand side of each label that he keeps in his apron. This works out to be every other slot for the entire three hundred to six hundred feet. The order-filler will approach each slot, tear off the shrink wrap from the pallet that has been placed there. The discarded shrink wrap, and any other trash, will be placed in gray buckets that are hanging from chains above the black, two or three foot wide rubber conveyer belt that runs through the middle of the module.

The order-filler will then stick one label on each box and place it on the conveyer line with the label and bar code up so that it can be scanned easier later. He will then move on to the next slot until that entire side is done; then move on to the next side of the first level, sign out more labels, and eventually move on to do both sides of the second level, and finish the batch on the third level.

The fourth level is called the "Accumulation Line." This is where the boxes pick up speed and travel across rollers instead of a rubber belt. The rollers will take the boxes out of the modules and across a virtual highway of four feet wide lines that fly through the rafters at great speed, and noise I might add.

After the order-fillers finish on the third level they place a square, red, plastic bucket after the last box and call in over the walkie-talkie radio that batch 23 is complete, then head down to the first level to start batch 24. The red "Batch Bucket" will help the Merge operator know when the last of everybody's freight has been shipped so he can start shipping the next batch.

The "Merge Operator" is the brains and muscle of the entire operation. He sits up high above the rest of the warehouse at the massive crossroads of conveyer lines and scans every box with a complex computer, sending it down the right line and hopefully on to the right truck that will deliver it to the stores.

Truck drivers will drop off their trailers and head for the break room for lunch until their next shipment is ready to go.

Outside, yard drivers pick up the empty trailers and deliver them to the next shipping dock door that has a vacancy and is ready to go. The next full trailer is picked up and hauled away. The truck driver is notified that it is ready, and off it goes to the store.

Inside, the shipping dock associate will write down the trailer number that the yard driver is bringing in, but at the same time can not shut off his line of freight because it might back up to Merge and cause all kinds of trouble. The shipping dock associate has two lights that look like a stoplight, one is green and the other is red. He *must* continually run his line and keep a green light. If he stops for any reason and the light turns red for too long, you have an assistant manager running over and jumping down your throat. If the yard driver is late bringing a trailer to your door, then the freight is thrown to the floor to keep the line moving.

Once the empty trailer arrives, the first items to be loaded are the "Non-Cons." This stands for non-conveyable; such as dog food which might rip on the conveyer line, or thirty two inch TVs that are too big for the lines, or even a whole pallet of one item that would be easier to ship together rather than break it down and ship every box independently.

After the non-cons are loaded, the shipping associate, or "Loader" punches a button and the line extends all the way into the trailer, within seconds, boxes are started down at a mile a minute.

The key now is to stack the freight as neatly as possible—and hustle! But this doesn't always happen, so the loader will stack the freight in a nice, neat wall, leaving about two feet at the top so he can throw freight behind it. When this is accomplished, he will move the line out and build another wall about two or three feet away from the last and throw boxes as fast as he can, filling up the space between. This technique is done until the truck is filled, shut, locked and shipped—then it's a race against time until you get a new trailer at your door.

The Shipping Dock has fifteen to twenty lanes. Lane thirteen is set aside for extras such as freight that slipped by Merge without being scanned or freight from a couple of the shipping lanes that fell behind. Every shipping lane has two or three people; one or two loading in the trailer itself and one outside the trailer that has to scan every single box that comes down the forty five degree angle belt line. Every box *must* be scanned before it enters the trailer, this slows the entire process down considerably, despite how many are in the trailer throwing boxes around. Several times I've seen assistant managers climbing halfway back through fully loaded trailers just to find one single box that didn't get scanned—it can be a real mess! Every item *has* to be accounted for.

Some warehouses have automatic scanners that scan every piece of merchandise before it is shipped.

Another aspect of the warehouse experience that I found very interesting was that the managers had little motorized carts they could zip around in. The carts were designed so that the driver had to stand up, but at the same time could pull two or three carts of freight from place to place if need be. I always wanted to drive one but I never had the opportunity. Loss Prevention (another name for security) would also drive these carts on their patrol around the warehouse, but mostly managers would use them to drive from module to module to check on progress.

There were two different module divisions in the warehouse; one was Case Lot and the other was the Distribution modules. Case Lot consisted of five modules: Alpha, Beta, Charlie, Delta and Echo. These modules held all of the regular freight that the stores carried every day such as bleach, hangers, motor oil, shampoo, etc.

The six Distribution modules: N, O, R, S, T and U, were half the size and held special orders along with large orders such as the hottest Christmas toys of the year that had to be sent out in large numbers. I was chosen to work in Case Lot and spent my first year in the Charlie module, and the last two years moving back and forth between Delta and Echo. I enjoyed it a lot except for the jams.

Jams were the frustrating moments when the freight would get stuck and crushed on the curved belts between the first and second, and third and forth levels. You would be standing on the first level innocently doing your work and here that spine tingling thud! Over time you learned to recognize that sound. You would then quickly pull the red emergency cord that ran along the belt and shut the entire module down, then spend the next thirty minutes cleaning up one giant mess.

Sometimes the jam would occur on the accumulation line as the freight was heading out to Merge. This would be extremely dangerous because at this point you couldn't shut the line down, you had to climb out on rapidly spinning rollers four stories up and try to readjust the crushed boxes with the momentum of other, heavier boxes pushing forward toward you. I guess you had to be good at roller skating to keep your balance.

Delta module had a very weak accumulation line, the line

heading out to Merge was fine, but boxes on Delta would just merely stop. I would be down on the first or second level and constantly hear Merge come over the intercom and say: "Delta! You have a jam on your accumulation line!" Then I would stop what I was doing and trek all the way up the stairs, push one little box two feet and get the line moving again, then trek all the way down again just in time to here Merge repeat his last page. Complaining didn't help, the maintenance crew would have had to put in an all new line and they weren't about to do that.

Talking to Merge was interesting, though. He would be our voice over the intercom if we were in the middle of the Module and couldn't get to a phone. We would get on our radios and say:

"Merge you got a copy?"
"Merge, go ahead."
"You got a batch bucket on Charlie!"
"10-4!"

Or

"Merge you got a copy?"
"Merge, go ahead."
"Yeah, we need a replenishment in Delta, slot D2794."

A few seconds later we would hear Merge paging our request. A "replenishment" was a signal for the forklift drivers to find the pelletized item for slot D2794 and bring it as quickly as possible to that slot in the module. The forklift drivers were good, sometimes they would bring the wrong item, but not very often.

Another module that I forgot to mention was the "Break-Pack Module." This module was mostly run by women and consisted of only single merchandise items that the stores only needed one of, such as, one pair of socks, or two small cans of paint, instead of a full case. These women would go down the row and throw all of these miscellaneous items into one box. After their order was filled, they would deliver and place these boxes onto the conveyer line of Charlie or Delta. Trust me, you didn't want these boxes breaking open in a jam and having small merchandise going everywhere.

Once, Merge was sending several break-pack boxes full of empty label backings from the order-fillers down lane thirteen so that they could be given to Loss Prevention and double checked to make sure every label had been accounted for, when suddenly the boxes jammed up, ripped open, and went flying in every direction. Empty label backings were everywhere up at Merge and almost shut the entire operation down. It was kind of funny to walk under the line and see the long, white streams of thin wax paper hanging down everywhere. From that day forward Loss Prevention decided to go around to every module and pick them up themselves instead of having Merge run them down the line to them.

After the break-pack boxes with merchandise were delivered to the stores, the stores had to return the empty boxes to the warehouse and save the company eighty cents per box.

Overall, I enjoyed working at the warehouse, it was the best paying job that I ever had, to date. And even though I was employed there after Mr. Sam Walton had passed away I never had the opportunity to meet or see any of the top Wal-Mart executives in the three years that I was working there, even though the warehouse was right there in Wal-Mart's hometown of Bentonville, Arkansas. The President and CEO at the time, Mr. David Glass, was once asked to come and give a talk, but turned the offer down so he could attend a golf game. Sometimes I don't fault his decision, we were a rambunctious crew. There was one time when someone had gotten mad, stormed into the bathroom, taken the lid off the back of the toilet, aimed the filler hose straight up in the air, flushed it and fled, leaving a stream of water hitting the ceiling and flooding the bathroom.

Ah, those were the days!

Chapter Four

POINTS TO PONDER

— It is well documented that Wal-Mart had been investigated a few years ago for using child labor in Saipan to manufacture clothing for just pennies a day, and then turning around and selling the clothes in the United States at a higher prophet margin. After the story broke, Wal-Mart introduced the Mary Kate and Ashley Olsen clothing line to cover up any wrong doing. Smart move. Who's going to accuse them of child labor now that they've signed a deal with the multi-million dollar teenage Olsen twins?

— Sam Walton called his managers "Servant Leaders."

— A national tragedy will not send people running because everybody wants to see what is going on. This is what Osama Bin Laden was hoping for—complete chaos; the stock market to crash. No such luck.

— The basis for most problems in society today is simply the fact that everyone is offended, and offended by the smallest things. "We can't have religion in schools." "We can't say the Pledge of Allegiance because it is worshiping idols." "My neighbor's house is the wrong color." "Eating fast food will make me fat."

The Webster's Dictionary defines the word "Offend" as

such: 1. To hurt the feelings of; insult. 2. To be displeasing to (the taste, sense, etc.).

If someone is doing something that you don't like, bring it to their attention like an adult and then drop it. But this problem has gone on for many years; if one neighbor has a beautiful lawn with hundreds of beautiful flowers, and the guy next door has piles of junk cars piled in his yard, remember that he might be an auto mechanic, an antique collector, or an off-the-wall artist that is into strange art. Most people don't think about such things, they only think about how bad the neighborhood looks based on their own opinion. So, many years ago, someone came up with the idea of putting up a fence between the two properties so that each neighbor could do what he or she wanted on their own property. So much for sharing. But that still didn't work because we still have that childhood mentality: "He's looking at me! Tell him to stop!"

It's time to grow up. If you don't like the junk cars next door then keep your mouth shut unless there is *Spillage*. Spillage is anything that crosses the fence line, such as rats or snakes that cross over into your flowers. Only then should something be done.

— Prevention and safety are out of control. Giving someone the power to oversee prevention or safety is a bad idea because it is a limitless power. The fact that something *might* happen can go on forever. We need to set basic guidelines and leave it at that—anything more is overkill, simply because nobody wants to get hurt; everybody can experience pain and pretty much knows what their limits are.

Any government agency that has been set up to regulate safety, such as OSHA, should be done away with. People should learn to think for themselves.

— The Sixteenth Amendment, concerning income tax, should be done away with. The IRS should also be done away with.

Most people say that we need taxes to pay for roads, schools and libraries, but that is not true because most public schools and libraries are privately funded anyway. As for roads, they are laid down and then dug right back up again because of a change in plans or to fix something that was done wrong in the first place.

Private and home school students perform much better on standardized tests. And most of the tax money for public education doesn't go to the students for better books or to buy new basketballs for the gym class, it goes directly into the pockets of superintendents that make upwards of $100,000 to $300,000 a year.

My grandmother was a school teacher in the 1940s to the 1950s. She heard the same old sayings even then: "We need more money for education."

If they don't have enough money by now, they never will.

— Have you ever noticed that tax day, April 15, and the elections that are held in early November are on the farthest points of the calendar? That was designed so that the general public would forget about paying taxes and would re-elect the same politicians right back into office. Let's see how many politicians would keep their jobs if election day was held on April 16.

— Wal-Mart has a 10 foot rule that requires all associates to greet any customer that comes within ten feet.

— Wal-Mart is one of the most wasteful companies in the world. Any general merchandise that is still operational but not sellable is thrown away. This also includes tomatoes or lettuce that have even the smallest brown spots, or eggs and milk that are only one day past their due date. Most of this problem is due to OSHA, but Wal-Mart has absolutely no problem discarding perfectly good merchandise instead of giving it away free to the needy because doing this act of kindness would cut into sales.

— If a Wal-Mart employee does something good in the community Wal-Mart will immediately take credit for it. "Hooray! He works for Wal-Mart!" Associates will never be on the same level as Mr. Sam, but you can live his dream! They'll even give you a button that says so.

— Wal-Mart doesn't purchase regularly priced merchandise and mark it lower than the competition, they purchase cheap merchandise and mark it way up, keeping it under the set price of the competition.

— Wal-Mart associates are not allowed to leave merchandise in shopping carts or sitting directly on the sales floor. If merchandise needs to sit on the floor, it is placed on a "Stack Base." A stack base is a black plastic pallet that is often set in the middle of the main action alley, and cosmetically looks better than a wooden pallet.

The theory of having two different types of merchandise sitting back to back on the stack base works just as well as the dump bins, i.e. a display of trash cans on one half and a display of laundry baskets on the other half—merchandise sells a lot faster using this method.

— When paging over the intercom, an associate is not allowed to use another associate's last name.

— Every few months stores undergo an evaluation for safety and set regulations. This evaluation is called "Star," or around Christmas time, is called "Snowflake." I believe that this evaluation is done by store managers from surrounding stores in the region, but one thing that is certain is that they will shake every aisle and see if anything will fall off of the risers.

— The number one stolen item at Wal-Mart in 2003 was baby formula.

— The "Buck-At-a-Time" program that Wal-Mart started features clip strips in front, or along side regular merchandise throughout the store. For example, if you are buying a toy for your child's birthday, there will be a thin, white or clear plastic strip that is holding twelve rolls of Scotch tape, which has been conveniently placed right next to the item that you are buying. This is perfect, since you probably need to buy tape anyway to wrap your child's gift.

Clip strips usually only feature inexpensive merchandise.

— There are two types of leaders in the government: Ones that expect people to do things for them, and ones that expect to do things for other people.

— Marking the sales price as 2 for $3.00, is a lot better than marking it as $1.50 each.

— Every associate carries a picture of Sam Walton with their name badge.

— A "Merit Raise" is only 2% to 5% of your current salary and

can be given only once a year, if you are in good standing with the company.
— A "Side Kick" is a small, silver metal display at the end of every aisle that features small, inexpensive merchandise.
— A lot of merchandise won't set off the alarms. Only electronics, clothes, condoms and some microwaves and vacuum cleaners have the ability.

Wal-Mart, however, is proposing to give every piece of merchandise a tag that can be tracked by satellite, even after it leaves the property. This distinctive new technology is called RFID (Radio Frequency Identification). It is designed to track any given piece of merchandise anywhere in the store. Each individual case or pallet will have its own unique tag and will be able to be located no matter where it is, so the shampoo in Oklahoma will be able to be told apart from the exact same toothpaste in Indiana. It's still just a matter of getting the department managers, or any other associates, to dig through the miscellaneous pallet in the backroom for you. Good luck!
— In a national election, only 20% of the people vote in the primaries, and 35% vote in the general election.
— More people watch the Super Bowl than vote.
— Most new law makers do just that—they make new laws. Nobody has ever thought about getting into office and repealing old or useless laws.
— The I.R.S. was only supposed to be temporary during World War II.
— The Press claims to be unbiased by using words like "Suspect," or "Alleged," but they never give equal time to third parties. Are they unbiased? No.
— In the legendary 2000 presidential election between George W. Bush and Al Gore. The deciding vote came down to the state of Florida. A debate arose about hanging chads on the paper ballots, and wether or not the voter wanted candidate A or candidate B. After several scientific tests were conducted, the result came back that the only way to have a hanging chad was to punch out two or more ballots at one time.
— In most trials, judges will allow only certain information to be revealed to the jury. I say, let the jury hear *every* piece of

information and then make an informed decision. For example, several years ago, a woman was downstairs in her basement and a man started walking down the stairs causing the lady to panic. She fired several rounds from her gun and killed the man instantly. The strange man turned out to be her husband and eventually the lady was released from custody after a trial because she was simply just trying to defend herself. Sound reasonable? No. because . . . *what the jury didn't hear*, was that this same lady had shot her first husband in almost the same manner.

Watch any news program such as Dateline, 60 Minutes or 20/20, and any time that the show discusses a trial anywhere in the nation, after the outcome you will always hear: "What the jury didn't hear . . ."

— When you are called to jury duty you have the American right to change the law that is being presented on trial. Think about it, if someone is being accused of a crime and the law says that person is guilty, then why do you need eight to twelve people to take time off from work to sit in a room together, nodding in agreement that the law finds them guilty. You don't. The law has been called into question, and for that brief moment, for that one particular instant, you are above the law. That is one of the many checks and balances that this country has. It was designed to rid the country of ridiculous laws. No judge would ever admit to this, but it is absolutely true.

— Government should earn their money like everyone else. If they have a huge project that they want to accomplish, they should save up for it like every other American.

— Public servant, a servant of the public.

— I personally think that the role of government should be simple. To illustrate my point more clearly, let's say that life is nothing more than one big highway. The role of the government should do just two things: Make sure everyone is obeying the speed limit, and make sure that everyone is driving on the right side of the street. That's it. The end. Period. But the government doesn't do that, they have to analyze what color cars are on the road; how many cars are on the road;

what types of cars are on the road; what kind of paint is used on every car; how wide are the steering wheels; what kind of rubber is used for the tires; how wide is the tread; how many passengers are in the car; what are their names and ages just in case they might commit a crime; what color is their hair; what kind of fabric is used for the seats; what color is the interior; how many stitches are sewn into the seatbelts; how much light is given off by the headlights; is the light yellow, white or blue; how many cup holders are dispensed throughout the vehicle . . .

It gets to be ridiculous.

— In the next election we should start using words like, "Hiring" and "Firing" rather than "Voting" or "Electing."

— Most local tax dollars go to finance the city government businesses such as their water and electrical power companies, etc. The government should shut down, get out of business for themselves and allow private companies to take over. That is what freedom is all about!

— Life carries on without the government. During hurricane Isabel and the massive blackouts in New York in 2002-2003, when the local government was completely shut down, people in the community got along great.

— Environmentalists should have to attend several years of school and be trained like doctors and lawyers.

— At Wal-Mart, associates are given an annual bonus based on how long they can go without an accident, and keeping shrinkage (lost or stolen merchandise) low.

— In the grocery department at Wal-Mart, they use words like, "Zoning" and "Facing up" to mean pulling cans or bottles forward so that the aisle looks cosmetically sound from a distance.

— You do not need a college degree to work your way up at Wal-Mart; however, those with a degree are chosen first to enter the internship training program.

— Wal-Mart does not allow any associate to work overtime—at all! If you end up working overtime on, let's say the fourth of July, you must schedule another day off in the same work week so that there is not more than forty hours in that particular pay period. Also, you must never work off the clock during your personal time.

— If a customer purchased a defective piece of merchandise from Wal-Mart, they should not call the store to find out how to fix it, they should call the manufacturer. I remember once receiving a call from a lady that had purchased a defective DVD player, she told me what brand it was and asked if I could fix it. I have never had training in repairing electronics so all I could do was advise her to bring it back to the store and exchange it, with the hope that her brand was still in stock and possibly worked better.

To avoid any confusion on this matter in the future, customers should buy electronics and other appliances from specialized dealers or electronic stores that have the maintenance ability to fix such items. Remember, if all else fails, call the manufacturer.

— A CSM (Customer Service Manager) is a cashier that has been promoted, and has the job duty to oversee all other cashiers with sale transactions, as well as any other problems that may arise. Their job level is still working under assistant managers.

— A "Flex aisle" or "Seasonal aisle" is an aisle that is used for different types of merchandise throughout the year. For example, it may contain Valentine bears for a couple of months, then summer plastic cups and dishes a few months later.

— Assistant managers and store managers are not from your local community as Wal-Mart would have you believe. They are brought in from other areas.

— People that are traveling through town with a camper trailer are allowed to stay in a Wal-Mart parking lot, but only for one night and you can't plug into Wal-Mart's electrical power. The same rule applies to truck drivers.

— Politicians are corrupt, that is common knowledge. But most problems today are strictly due to the voters themselves; most don't vote, and those that do, only vote straight Party. They walk in to a voting booth and hit one button—straight Republican, or straight Democrat. They're not even sure which candidate that they voted for, at least until after the election.

If Hitler were alive today and ran for governor in the state of Utah as a republican, he would win instantly and nobody would know until it was too late.

"Republican? That's good enough for me!"

— In Utah, a protester that was standing outside protesting the Salt Lake City 2002 Olympic bribery trial (in which Tom Welsh and Dave Johnson were accused of handing out bribes) was given a ticket because he didn't have a permit from the General Services Administration.

What happened to freedom of speech? He was only standing there singing comedy songs while strumming a guitar.

He also received a citation for standing on the sidewalk which is federal property—it is no longer public property.

— Do we have freedom of the press? No. Broadcasters have to obtain a license from the FCC (Federal Communications Commission). Stations receive licenses only when the FCC judges it to be "in the public interest, convenience, or necessity." Licenses are granted for a limited period, and the FCC may choose not to renew. The FCC has never defined what the "public interest" means. In the past, it preferred a case by case approach, which has been called, "regulation by raised eyebrow."

— Security? What if terrorists disguised their guns as cameras or other tourist devices? What if terrorists made guns from plastic so that they couldn't be picked up by metal detectors?

— Wal-Mart is trying so hard to look like part of your local community that they invented the "Neighborhood Market," which is nothing more than a smaller Wal-Mart store.

— Wal-Mart's use of the word "S.W.A.S." stands for "Store Within A Store." The word was designed to make department managers think like individual retail outlets.

— Wal-Mart associates are not allowed to wear blue jeans.

— How do we know that the Wal-Mart buyers aren't investing in stocks of small companies that manufacture the products that they sell? That would be pure profit.

Take for example, the Rocket. The Rocket is a new cart that associates wheel out onto the sales floor to help stock shelves. A buyer would merely have to suggest to a friend or family member that several million units had been made and will be in stores by such and such a date. No one would ever know.

— The government uses money to dictate to people. If the government doesn't want a citizen to do something, such as going into business for themselves, or they want to run you out of town, they will simply raise the price of land, tax, or impose impact fees.

— The government and courts have the laws so messed up that nobody really knows what's legal and what's not.

— Voting for other parties besides Republicans and Democrats is not throwing your vote away. If everyone voted that normally didn't vote, it *would* make a difference.

— It is time for this country to grow up. We had our teenage, experimental era in the sixties, but now it's time to act like adults.

— We have a great country! The greatest country in the world! It is not in ruins, but we need to stand up and protect the constitution before it's too far gone. We can't let it slip away.

Chapter Five

STORM

On October 23, 2003, INS agents (Immigration Naturalization Services) arrested three hundred illegal workers in an immigration crackdown at sixty Wal-Mart stores in twenty one states. The workers were members of cleaning crews hired by outside contractors and Wal-Mart was rumored to know all about their illegal status.

No action was taken against Wal-Mart except for nine of the undocumented workers that have filed a class-action lawsuit on behalf of thousands of workers, both legal and illegal. The lawsuit claims the company systematically deprived the employees of labor-law protection, which included depriving them of insurance benefits, worker's comp and even overtime pay (Wal-Mart will *not* pay overtime for any reason).

Weren't the federal authorities supposed to be going after Wal-Mart?

Instead of penalizing the management that was allegedly exploiting and abusing the employees, federal agents arrested the alleged victims. Instead of going after the operators of the private maintenance companies or the ultra rich Walton family, the feds went after the lowly maintenance workers. Wal-Mart took advantage of the fact that because some people are here in this country without the proper immigration papers, they won't complain.

Many of those arrested in the immigration raids were mothers and fathers working hard to provide for their families. Some of them might have children they want to put in college so that they don't have to scrub toilets when they grow up.

But why exactly did the government arrest these people? There are three main reasons:

1. Ignorance. In states such as New Mexico, among many others, illegal residents are allowed to have a driver's license, and are first to receive financial aid for homes and schools.
2. To show power. The federal government loves to conduct raids to "make an example" out of anyone who crosses their path.
3. Panic. It is common knowledge that the government now owns many of the major airlines, since most have filed for bankruptcy and the government was there to buy them out through financial aid, not to mention the fact that they completely took control over security. But now the government is turning Washington D.C. into a fortress.

An anti-aircraft missile, ready for immediate use, sits atop a federal office building near the White House. Devices that test the air for chemical and biological substances are positioned throughout the city. Subway stations are now equipped with bomb containment trash bins. A major highway that runs by the Pentagon is being rerouted several hundred yards away. A security wall is going up around the Washington Monument.

Day by day the nation's capital, which was once an elegant city known for its graceful beauty, is quickly becoming and armed camp.

By now, most federal buildings and monuments have prodigious security measures in place, with enhancements planned or all ready underway.

Police officers with dogs trained to sniff out explosives are stopping cars before they drive past the Capital. Plans have been approved to build a security perimeter around the ten buildings of the Smithsonian Institution and the Department of Agriculture.

The interiors of most government buildings have taken on aspects of an airport, with magnetometers at every entrance and a greater presence of law enforcement officers. The entrance to the Washington Monument has metal detectors and X-ray machines, as does the front door of the Botanical Garden greenhouse at the foot of Capital Hill.

Is this still the people's land?

Chapter Six

THE LAND OF AMERICA

"I know something about being a government. And you've got a good one."
—*George W. Bush, campaigning for Governor Mike Huckabee; Bentonville, Arkansas; November 4, 2002*

"They misunderestimated me."
—*George W. Bush in Bentonville, Arkansas; November 6, 2000*

Excerpts from, "Bushisms: The accidental wit and wisdom of our 43rd President." Andrews McMeel Publishing.

In April of 2002 I flew to New York City to meet with the buyers from the Barnes and Noble bookstores and give them a pitch for my new science fiction novel. They were very nice people, but the meeting didn't turn out to be as productive as I had planned, so I held my chin up high and walked out the door with my briefcase and headed down the street.

My intention now was to go sightseeing since I had never been to New York before. I made my way to Grand Central Station and boarded the nearest subway car; I really didn't care where it went or where I ended up because I could merely hail a taxi cab and return to my hotel.

The train swiftly took me to streets, buildings and allowed me to meet people that I had never seen before. It was so interesting. Jumping from train to train I saw such sights as Time Square, Broadway, the Brooklyn Bridge, and I even took a bus to see the Statue of Liberty.

Then I arrived at Ground Zero, the sight of the World Trade Center bombings. The disaster had only happened eight months earlier, and even though some time had passed, I still witnessed young, teenage girls crying.

For crowd control you had to have a ticket to go up a long, wooden ramp to the outlook, but I was told the tickets were available at the peer down by the ocean, so I made my way through more streets and people until I came to the ticket booth and picked up one free ticket, and headed back.

The sight of the clean up was stunning; the group I was with was silent; I snapped a couple of photographs and after five minutes the usher escorted us back down the ramp so that the next group could arrive.

I spent the rest of the day doing more sightseeing until, around midnight, when I found myself back on a virtually empty train that had come to a dead end, obviously the end of its tracks. I got off and watched as the train left from the same direction that it had come from.

I walked up to the street and there I was again, at Ground Zero. Only this time there was no outlook, I was there, directly on the sight. I was walking around on the torn street watching the clean up crew, and what I like to call the 9/11 workers, cleaning up the very last of the debris.

Even after eight months there were still several bodies that were unaccounted for, which gave the warm night air a feeling of eeriness. At the same time, a light fog, or possibly smoke, had settled in and gave the atmosphere a relaxing calmness.

The workers didn't say anything to me and carried on with their work. I walked around a few minutes more, said a short prayer, took one last glance back at the sight and made my way back down to the subway and waited for the next train to arrive. I left with a memory that I will never forget.

As lasting as those memories will be for me, the flight to and from New York was a whole different story. I flew out of Salt Lake City, Utah, transferred flights in Phoenix, Arizona, and then took a six hour flight directly to New York.

My father drove me to the Salt Lake airport and walked me inside to say goodbye, but once inside we found so much security there that it was simply unbelievable; where there had once been a calm, rational atmosphere that allowed family members to escort passengers to the gates, we now found that family had to wait at the baggage check-in while passengers had to make their way through a series of military check points, complete with armed guards and police dogs.

I said goodbye to my father, checked my bags in, and headed through security. I went through the standard metal detectors, and noticed up ahead that they were making everybody take off their shoes so that they could search in vain for obsolete shoe bombs. I waited patiently in line until it was my turn; the security guard finished with the gentleman in front of me and then turned in my direction and gave me a very strange look.

"Are you waiting for somebody?" he asked.

"Uh, no," I said in shock. "I just thought that you wanted me to . . ."

"No, just go ahead sir."

"Uh, um, okay."

For some odd reason I didn't have to go through the security that everyone else had to. The same thing was true at the gate just before we boarded the plane, they pulled aside a nice old lady and two young Hispanic boys that had been standing right in front of me, and commenced searching through their carry-on luggage, while I was allowed to board free and clear. I didn't get it. It seemed to me that their rational thinking was a bit misconstrued. I mean, to be completely honest, I, a twenty something man, would probably be a more likely candidate as a terrorist than two preteen boys or a nice old lady in her mid eighties to early nineties.

At any rate, after seeing the Salt Lake airport fly off the deep end, I was scared to death to see what a mess the New York airport had become. But, again, I was thoroughly surprised. When I flew out of New York back to Utah I was surprised to find that the New

York airport had kept some sensibility, at least for the time being. Security was a bit tighter, but there were no armed guards; no soldiers with police dogs—and that was the city that had been under attack!

Only a year later, however, after the government had taken over all airport security, and all of the major airlines, thinking that they could run a better operation, did I see everything go down hill just as I had seen with similar results at the Salt Lake airport.

At the Tulsa airport, there would be no getting through security with a piece of mind this time; they had me stand in line for an hour or more just to have my shoes inspected; they checked out every last piece of metal, including a brief moment when two security guards had to determine that the metal that was setting off the alarm was just the staples in my checkbook.

For now, the citizens are going along with the motions—the scrutiny of going through security, the boarding of the plane, the un-boarding and rechecking of bags because someone had made a joke about a box knife. But sometime down the road the people will say enough is enough! And then, and only then, will this nation start to mature.

*　　*　　*

In 1986 I attended Grace Hill Elementary School in Rogers, Arkansas, the town right next door to Bentonville and the location of the very first Wal-Mart. One day as I was packing items in my backpack and was about to head home, I received word from my teacher that then Vice President George Bush Sr. was coming to the Rogers Youth Center to give a speech. I had my mom drop me off at the youth center so that I could attend. The news of George Bush's arrival was given out on such short notice that my mother couldn't stay because she had other planned errands to run; I even overheard two ladies talking in the parking lot:

"What's going on?" one asked.

"Vice President Bush is going to give a speech."

"Really, I just saw a huge crowd of people gathered here and wanted to see what was going on."

I went inside and found that there was absolutely no security. I took a seat at the highest point at the venue which held about five hundred people, mostly just local citizens that wanted to watch their sons play basketball. No banners or any other fanfare had been placed on display, only a small, brown, wooden stage in the corner of the basketball court with a large American flag draped majestically behind it.

I waited roughly one hour until the Vice President's scheduled arrival time and slowly began to get a headache. By the time he was supposed to arrive my head was throbbing and no one knew how much longer it would be. I waited an additional twenty minutes or so and decided that since I didn't have any medication on me that it was time to go home. I called my mother and had her come pick me up; the last thing I remember was crashing on my grandmother's bed and sleeping for several hours. That evening my family and I went out for a nice dinner, so the day wasn't a complete loss.

The newspaper the next day reported that the Vice President was forty five minutes late. Years later when President George Bush came to Bentonville to award Sam Walton the Medal of Freedom in 1992, the newspaper reported that this visit was the first time he had come to northwest Arkansas. I know for a fact that wasn't true.

*   *   *

If the truth be known, I always had a lot of fun working the night shift at Wal-Mart. One night, after the store was closed, I was helping out a coworker named Tracy in the infants department. We had a ladder set up and I was hanging merchandise on the top row of the peg hooks that had been affixed to the outside of the nearby dressing rooms.

As most customers know, the dressing rooms do not go all the way to the ceiling and have an open top. All at once I heard my name being called. I looked across the tops of the dressing rooms toward the housewares department and saw Intern Steve looking for me.

"Grant! Where are you?!"

Thinking quickly I said the first thing that came to my mind. "I'm above the women's dressing room!"

I thought Tracy was about to die laughing.

GRANT LEE

*   *   *

Now, let me get to the heart of this chapter, appropriately titled "The land of America." That is a significant title because that is what America is all about, the right to own land.

If you currently own an acre or two and have nothing more than a deed to your land, you are more than likely paying property tax, which is essentially the same as paying rent, and the government is your landlord. Through such departments as Planning and Zoning, the government can tell you what your home and property should look like and what changes you can make to it. But there is no need to worry because all you need is a Land Patent.

In 1871 the Congress of the United States of America passed the Land Patent Act. This allows all citizens to have complete sovereignty over their land, this is *absolute* title to your land.

Land Patents are all ready in place for you, all you have to do is declare publicly that the land is yours. First you apply for a certificate from the Bureau of Land Management (BLM) at a cost of around two dollars to four dollars. Next, you write a short, detailed description of your land (trees, dirt, hills, grass, etc.), including a brief description of your house and belongings (which must be declared as "Homestead"). In other words, a Land Patent is for the land and a Homestead is for your house. After the descriptions have been written, you must run them, along with your certificate number, in the local newspaper three times consecutively, depending on the laws of your state. This ad will give anyone time to challenge your claim to the land, if no one does, you get a signed statement from the newspaper and file your claim with the city or county recorder in your area, and the land is yours.

This same method of obtaining a Land Patent should be about the same in every state; the fourteenth amendment of the Constitution basically states that all laws throughout the land must be equal.

But, I should warn you that local governments do not like giving out Land Patents. They feel that tax payers are their magical money tree, and without the tax dollars and the right to tell you what to do, they are at a loss. As I said earlier in this book, the government should save up and earn money for projects that they want to complete just like every other American.

Your local government may even try to hold benefits from you such as water, electricity, etc. until you give up your Land Patent, at which time you can sue the city on the grounds of harassment. If you receive water and electricity from a private company then you have nothing to worry about. I just hope nothing like this happens to you.

You should also *never* sign a waiver to your land. For example, if the city wants to run a sewer through your land you may allow them to do so but do not sign a waiver! This will call your sovereignty into question and you will lose all rights to your patent.

Though you do have *complete* control of your land there are still some things that you can't do such as cause damage to your neighbor's property. If rain were to run off your roof and destroy the neighbor's flower garden then you might want to fix the problem, you do have to be kind to others.

Always remember the Golden Rule: "Do unto others as you would have them do unto you."

The reason that I am so adamant about Homestead and Land Patents is because I knew a lady once that wanted to build an addition on to her house. She completed all of the appropriate paper work and received permission from the junior home inspector, and thus began work digging out a basement on the south side of her house. The job was coming along beautifully; she had the cement walls in place and was about to begin work on the upstairs when all of a sudden the senior home inspector showed up. He insisted that she could only build on the north side of her house. So, she filled in her basement with dirt and started building on the north side. That doesn't sound so bad does it? But, the fact was, there was nothing on the north side of her house, she lived on the edge of a hill that dropped straight down. She did complete the work and now has two extra bedrooms that are six feet by six feet wide and twenty five foot high ceilings—and no basement. All of this harassment could have been prevented if she had just filed for a Land Patent!

If you wanted to build a house that looked just like a giant ice cream cone, you would have the right!

We must all stand up for what we believe in! It isn't easy, but it must be done. That is why the National Anthem ends with a question mark in most song books.

" . . . land of the Free, and home of the Brave?"

Other books written by Grant Lee include the science fiction novel, *The Great Time-Link Photography Project*, and an off-the-wall comedy entitled, *Instru-Mental*.

Coming soon, the new edition of *Microworlds: Atom Force*, including the long lost missing chapter.

grantleebooks@geocities.com

Printed in the United States
31688LVS00003B/265-276

9 781413 454123